# Loving Couples

Designs to Inspire Your Creative Genius

Published in 2015 by Global Insight Productions

Illustrated by Ewelina Terczynska

Creative Director Rosa MeChel

www.BeHappyColoringBooks.com

ISBN: 978-0-9796942-7-1

# Join Our Creative Community
## BeHappyColoringBooks.com

For your coloring and painting pleasure,
if you have creative genius ideas that you
would like for our artist to design, let us know.

We also want you to be a part of our Be Happy
Art Gallery. So go ahead and send us your
masterpiece and we will share it with the world.

You can contact us at **info@behappycoloring.com**

 facebook.com/behappycoloring

 pinterest.com/behappycoloring

 Instagram.com/behappycoloring

 twitter.com/behappycoloring

# Be Happy Coloring Books

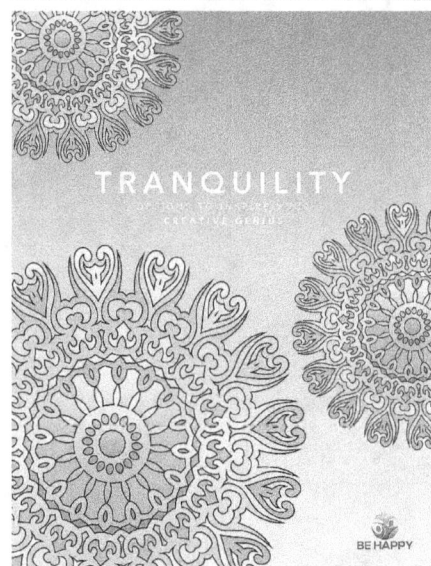

Stay tuned, more coloring books to come.
Our artists are passionately creating
new coloring pages to help inspire
your creative genius.

**www.BeHappyColoringBooks.com**